Changing Circumstances

Changing Circumstances
An Acting Manual with 24 Scenes

Lorinne Vozoff

HEINEMANN
Portsmouth, NH

Heinemann
A division of Reed Elsevier Inc.
361 Hanover Street
Portsmouth, NH 03801–3912
www.heinemanndrama.com

Offices and agents throughout the world

Performance rights information can be found on p. 79.

Library of Congress Cataloging-in-Publication Data
Vozoff, Lorinne.
    Changing circumstances : an acting manual with 24 scenes /
by Lorinne Vozoff.
      p. cm.
    ISBN 0-325-00293-2 (alk. paper)
     1. Acting. I. Title.
    PN2080.V69 2000
    792'.028—dc21   00-029583

Editor: Lisa A. Barnett
Production: Sonja S. Chapman
Cover design: Joni Doherty Design
Manufacturing: Louise Richardson

Printed in the United States of America on acid-free paper
04 03 02 01 00 DA 1 2 3 4 5

For Kate and Deon.

And dedicated to
all true actors in the world.

Contents

Introduction IX

PART I. THE PRINCIPLES OF THE SYSTEM 1
Training and Technique 3

PART II. THE SCRIPTS 23
Chris and Sage 25
Fren and Joey 32
Lan and Lesley 38
Pat and Mickey 44
Fom and Kad 52
Haser and Fondi 57
Padd and Roth 65
Ash and Bolli 71

Introduction

Acting is the search for the soul, nothing less than a sublime quest for the deepest, truest part of ourselves. Applied to a worthy script, fine acting can express the intriguing range of emotions that spring from our collective human condition. It transcends time and culture to show not only what separates us from one another but, more important, what eternally makes us all the same. A trained and inspired actor lets us understand both a fourteenth-century Italian monk and a contemporary Russian prostitute because their passions are so analogous to our own.

I have been acting for many years. Along the way, I have performed with many gifted partners. I can assure you, nothing is more exhilarating than working with a generous and talented actor. When the chemistry is right and the emotions flow effortlessly, it is as if acting were the easiest thing in the world. But I learned early on that we are rarely this lucky. During the early years of my career, my own acting ability was an elusive mystery to me. My best performances were unpredictable. I could never trust that I would be able to repeat them. I wondered if the Muse might abandon me the next time, leaving me to flounder on stage without purpose.

Then, in 1970, I had the great good fortune to meet Jack Garfein and, later, the legendary Harold Clurman at what was then The Actors and Directors Lab, an acting school in Los Angeles. Up until that point, I had trained as most actors do: college courses, workshops, voice training, movement and dance classes. I had already worked in community theatre, repertory companies, summer stock, and both film and television. Still, in retrospect, I see that my real, best training did not begin until I heard Garfein's opening lecture, which clarified the work of the

Russian acting teacher Constantin Stanislavski. Suddenly, I realized the reasons for the uncertainty I had been feeling about my work for so long. I saw that while I was talented enough to give some solid performances, I lacked the technique necessary to understand and repeat them.

So, under Garfein's careful and sometimes painful instruction, and with periodic critique and input from Clurman, my true acting education began in earnest. I spent five years working at The Lab, immersed in Stanislavski's System. I took as many classes as I could handle; I took some of them twice. And one class, called "Objectives," I took a third time because Garfein encouraged me to. "Take it again, Lorinne," he said. "Don't let there be any doubt in your mind about how to use this essential part of the System." He was right, of course. During those five years I learned how to find the truth—inside myself and within a good script. I learned how to use that truth and how to own it on stage.

For the past twenty years, I also have been an acting teacher. Early on, I realized a great many students have difficulty internalizing the basic principles of the Stanislavski System, which I teach. It sometimes seemed that no matter how often we reviewed the material, and despite their wonderfully crafted essay answers to final exam questions, my students still had trouble getting on stage and working with a clear purpose in mind. They were often unable to provide their acting partner with a problem. Most of all, they could not take a series of distinct actions—specific, nameable verbs that they might try in the effort to overcome their problem and accomplish their objective on stage.

Of course, I have to admit that a part of me felt slightly vindicated by their trouble. I was not the only one who found this a challenge, I thought to myself. I may have needed to take that "Objectives" course three times, but so did some other genuinely talented actors. Still, the teacher in me kept trying to devise a more efficient way to impart the information. Like almost every other school of thought, Stanislavski's System is beautifully clear and simple—once you understand it. Wasn't there, I kept asking myself, some effective tool for conveying it to students?

The longer I taught, the more certain I became that a major problem for acting students (even the best ones) was the scripts they were assigned. Great plays—like *Othello, The Doll's House, The Glass Menagerie, Bus Stop, The Homecoming*—are such rich and complex works that it's easy to get sidetracked or waylaid by one's enthusiasm for the sweep of the entire piece. Many students simply found it impossible to successfully identify and present the objectives, problems, and actions that applied to isolated scenes.

Another problem centered on the issue of emotional intensity. Often, students are eager to work on the "crescendo" scenes from respected plays, for example, the tomb soliloquies from *Romeo and Juliet* or the confrontation between Biff and Willie that occurs toward the end of *Death of a Salesman*. Or they're assigned a scene from one of Harold Pinter's plays or something by Sam Shepard, where feelings either are obsessively kept in check or processed through a filter of utter emotional dysfunction. Granted, all good actors must arrive at the point where they can tackle work of this sort. But it's a lot to ask for students to cut their artistic teeth on such material.

How, for example, can any young actors (especially inexperienced ones) be expected to play the final scene between Desdemona and Othello? The emotions required for that scene are so intense! How can two people just learning to act successfully interpret *Betrayal*'s scene about control that takes place between a couple married for fifteen years, caught in a web of infidelity? Work like this calls for a level of maturity and life experience that are rarely found in young people. These scenes also require a full grasp of the plays in which they are found. And so, without those "legs" to stand on, it is extremely difficult for even the most talented students to make their work believable. I found myself feeling ridiculous when I asked my students to attempt such an assignment and embarrassed for them when they brought such material to me on their own.

So, I began writing short scenes for my students. The purpose was simple: to create "playlets" that would make it easy for them to work with the Stanislavski principles. I wrote these scenes as two-character pieces. Each character could be played by either a man or a woman, and each scene could be played three different ways while the dialogue remained the same. For example, one piece might be directed first as an encounter between strangers on an elevator, second as a conversation between an employee and boss, and third as an exchange between lovers in bed. Because the roles were interchangeable, each actor was offered a total of six parts per playlet.

Happily, I found that the scenes worked marvelously well. For one thing, each playlet let me assign work to six students instead of just two. That was a great advantage in large classes. Or, if I was working with a particularly small group, I could ask the same two students to do the scene in three completely different ways. This not only entertained the entire group, but it also provided a tremendous opportunity for the working students to experience dialogue as something flexible and open to creative interpretation. Most important of all, the scenes took students straight to the heart of objective, problem, and action. This gives the actor the experience of using Stanislavski's method successfully: They clearly lay out what each character wants, what the character is up against in trying to get it, and how the character behaves in an effort to get his or her needs satisfied.

I deliberately developed the *changing circumstances* in each playlet to evolve from the most straightforward to the most complex. As in the example above, there's rarely much intensity between strangers who interact in an elevator. But we up the emotional ante when we apply the same dialogue to a conversation between employee and boss. And we up it even more when those same words are exchanged between lovers in bed.

By no means are the circumstances in this book final or exclusive. I fully expect teachers to fine-tune the circumstances somewhat, or alter them more significantly if necessary, based on the makeup and sophistication of the students in any given class or workshop. What is important is that the basic concept remains intact and is clearly communicated to students: That acting technique, at its essence, consists of three elements—objective, problem, and action.

Perhaps it should not go without saying that my aim has been to make this book down-to-earth and extremely practical. Most of all, I have tried to ensure that it abide by that age old dictum: *become by doing.* Acting is an elevated art form, but it is also a craft. As such, it is best learned not by reading or writing or even watching those best at it. Instead, acting is most fully and profoundly grasped in the ritual of performing. By providing readers with Part I, a short primer that lays out the essential elements of the System's technique and then, in Part II, creating scripts that offer the experience of exactly how that technique is applied to real scenes and actual character development, I hope this book makes a meaningful and exciting contribution to actors' training. My aim is that it will demystify acting even as it honors the art of performance.

Speaking for myself, I have been abundantly rewarded for my efforts to learn Stanislavski's System. Now when I look at a script or review a few pages of audition dialogue, I know what to do. I know how to work. Quite simply, because I grasp the System and know how to apply it, I can call myself a trained professional. And that gives me no small measure of confidence. I am forever grateful for the gift of having learned this technique, and I am thankful for the many creative people and marvelous plays that have showed me the way to an art form that so deeply fulfills me. It is my hope that *Changing Circumstances* will help other actors find their way.

PART I

The Principles of the System

Training and Technique

It is sometimes said that great actors are born, not taught. Certainly no amount of training or technique can adequately compensate for what fate can provide. Talent is without substitute. It alone distinguishes between skill and greatness.

Still, we would be foolish to underestimate the importance of technique. In fact, I would argue that it is indispensable because it insures a departure point, a place from which to begin working as you wait for inspiration to come. This applies to everything from cooking to high art. There are some natural geniuses, but they are rare. There was only one Picasso. Not very many of us can pick up a guitar and start playing like Segovia. However, talent must be trained, and those who have mastered technique are simply better than those who have not.

Training gives an actor confidence, and there is nothing you need more when you go out on stage than the confidence that you know what you are going out there to do. Remember when you were a child and, perhaps, performed in a piano recital? Or recited a poem for an audience? Or did anything that required knowledge beforehand of what you were going to do? You were taught by someone, and that knowledge was what allowed you to walk out in front of an audience and do what you had been trained to do. Without training and practice, you would have been forced to hope that talent alone would carry you through the scrutiny of a public performance. We have all had the experience of being trapped in our seat in a darkened theatre, watching an actor who has no idea what he is doing. And if that makes us uncomfortable, how much worse must it be for that poor actor? A solid technique prevents this, and later, as we become more seasoned, it continues to support us. If the Muse fails to sing for us on a given night, we will not fall on our faces. Even when acting becomes second nature, when the process recedes into the subconscious, technique gives us the ability to measure our own creative progress. If we run into trouble, when we get lost in a part (as all actors sometimes do), it becomes the road map back to solid ground.

Many very talented young actors fear that a specific approach will inhibit their creativity. "I don't want to be taught any kind of craft," they will say. "I just want it to happen." That is all well and good until, on some fateful night, "it" does not happen. What then? Do you announce quite sheepishly, "No Play Tonight," and send the ticket holders home? Or do you go ahead and give a bad performance? Every audience deserves to see a play or film at its best, and that includes seeing you, the actor, at your best. With a solid technique, you can deliver, night after night, take after take. You will not disappoint your audience or yourself.

It has been my experience that technique *leads* the way to inspiration. It frees you to be genuinely creative. After all, if your energy goes into the panic of being on stage without knowing for certain what you are going to do, it is virtually impossible for inspiration to happen. On the other hand, when you are confident that, no matter what, you will know how to perform, it is much easier to relax. And relaxation is essential to inspiration.

There are also those actors who like to think of themselves a bit like baseball players about to step up to the plate in hopes of hitting a home run. Certainly, the thrill of spontaneous artistry is intoxicating. But there is a fundamental difference between batting and acting. Batting is improvisational; it is not an art form. Art is calculated; it is not an accident. As a professional actor, you know the line that will be addressed to you. And in rehearsal, by using the technique explored in this book (either with a director's help or even on your own), you will know what to do when the lights come up or the director shouts, "Action." You will know why you are out there. You will know what to expect. You will understand what it is that you are supposed to do. You will be relaxed and confident, and inspiration will come.

I want to state here, at the beginning, that I have not invented the principles that you will learn about in this book. Everything is rooted in the work and teachings of Constantin Stanislavski, an actor, director, and teacher who worked in Russia at the turn of the last century. Even more to the point, Stanislavski invented nothing. He simply defined a process that all good actors have gone through since the early Greeks formalized drama. His System is designed to help you find in yourself that which is analogous to the character you are interpreting. As a result, his technique allows you to sidestep clumsy attempts at "pretending." Stanislavski's work teaches us that good acting is anything but adding on false layers. It is removing all extraneous layers until you find the part of your real self that is like the character.

Put simply, the System asks you to share your true self with your audience. In order to do that, it asks you to be completely honest with yourself. What do you believe in? What do you stand up for? What is your standard? Who are you? Ask yourself these questions. Once you have begun to formulate the answers, be happy with the portrait you uncover. You are unique. You cannot be duplicated. There is only one of you in the whole world. Know, too, that whoever you are, whatever you are, you cannot hide it from your audience. Not if you do truthful acting. We are going to see you anyway. You are going to reveal yourself through your work. So, like the great actors of every generation, know what your essential quality is, and respect it. Be thoroughly yourself and nobody else. After all, it is *you* we want to see.

I would like to point out that technique is perhaps most useful to the very talented. Those who are most gifted seem to respond to the natural correctness of Stanislavski's System. Even before they have mastered the System—while they are in that frustrating limbo between understanding it but not yet being able to consistently apply it—gifted actors intuit that it can lead them to the truth inside their character, to the message of a good script. So as you work through all that follows, I hope you will remain invigorated. Rest assured that your effort will pay off in the end. And, with luck, you will be one of those all-too-rare artists who combines genuine talent with excellent technique. If so, then to see you work will be both a delight and a privilege.

The Magic "If"

Every actor, the beginner as well as the more experienced professional, confronts a perplexing question. What do you do when you are cast in a part that you cannot relate to? What if, at age 40, you are in a repertory company and cast as a 20-year-old or an 80-year-old? You would have to say either "I've forgotten that experience," or "I haven't had it yet." What if you are a young actor lucky enough to be cast as Hamlet? In their heart of hearts, most young men would have to say, "Hey, I've never been a prince. I've never had an uncle murder my father and then marry my mother. I've never wanted to kill anybody. How am I going to work on Hamlet?" These are not ridiculous questions. In fact, it is the actor with integrity and a sense of truth who is first to ask them.

Fortunately for us all, Stanislavski offers concrete advice: Find the magic "if." What would you do "if" . . . that happened to you? Again, there is a dilemma. Most drama is based on highly-charged circumstance. After all, the details of ordinary life do not form the basis of many plays or film scripts. So to ask what you would do if your mother and uncle fell in love behind your father's back and the uncle plotted his murder feels a bit far-fetched for most of us. So, Stanislavski said, use an analogous "if." Find whatever is analogous to that character in your own life. Draw an analogy between Hamlet's desire to kill Claudius and what you would want to do if someone tried to hurt someone you love. Think about it. This man has destroyed Hamlet's mother. He has turned her into a sex-crazed, vain, frail human being when she had once been a cherished, loyal wife and queen to a nation. This is what Claudius has done to Gertrude. Now, how would you feel about a man who did that to your mother?

If you say, "Well, I could never play the aspect of Hamlet that actually wants to kill Claudius." Maybe, and maybe not. According to some experts, we all have experienced every emotion there is by the time we reach 13, including the urge to kill. Children are unin-hibited and pure—if they feel something, you know it. It is only as we get older that we learn to conceal our feelings. So if the appro-priate feeling does not exist in your present life, go back to your childhood. Emotional gold is buried there. It is fertile ground for *remembered emotion* —a building block to all acting. Were you ever very angry at someone? Even if it was for just a second, did you ever want to do something physically violent to someone? Maybe to a bully on the playground, or to a friend who disappointed you. Start there and enlarge on that memory.

If I, as the teacher or director, ask you under what circumstances you would feel the urge to kill someone, you well might answer, "None. There are no circumstances that would make me want that. I don't think anyone should get violent under any conditions. And even if someone walked up and tried to hurt me, I wouldn't do any-thing." (I think that is doubtful; however, the director's job is to help an actor explore the possibilities.) Well, what if someone threatened your child? Or your mother? What if someone was trying to kill your sister? Do you think you could react to that? Most of us love someone enough that, even if we would not defend *ourselves* from an attack, we would become violent if that loved one were attacked. Once you find the analogous "if," you can work. The circumstances of the play or the film give you the basis of "if." But the impetus to act, to behave, has to be real. It must come from inside of you.

As another example, let's say that you have been cast as Ophelia. But you probably have never been engaged to a prince, loved him, and been rejected by him. So what do you use as an analogy? Well, what if, when you were 15, your boyfriend suddenly seemed uninterested in you. In particular, what if he waited until you were in public and, for no apparent reason, behaved as though he did not care about you? This is a theme in the lives of many teenage girls, partly because it seems to be human nature for some teenage boys to behave in this way. But as the young girl, you prob-ably did not understand why this was happening. Why, out of nowhere, did your boyfriend reject you? This may seem minor compared to what Ophelia experiences when Hamlet turns from her, but it is analogous nonetheless. Like you during your teens, Ophelia does not understand what has gone wrong. So return to those adolescent memories, because once you find your way to a genuine experience of extreme disappointment and rejection in romantic love, you can act Ophelia.

An actor's search for the analogous experience also (and most certainly) applies to positive passions. For example, it is safe to assume that we have all been in love. It usually first happens between the ages of 12 and 16. Living only for our love's attention, the delightful anticipation of being together, a certainty that only we two understand the depth of our commitment—these are the feelings that accompany that kind of young love, love that disregards all risk and defies any disapproval. In this, of course, we have the seeds of *Romeo and Juliet*. And very few of us would have to dig too deep if we were cast as one of the legendary lovers. We know in our hearts what we would do in those circumstances: risk all for the one we love.

Having acknowledged the importance of possessing strong passions, it is time for me to add a big "but." Yes, it is wonderful, in fact essential, to find analogous feelings. But never, ever *try* for the feeling, or try to *express* the feeling. If you do, you will get a cliché. Even a great actor would. If you need to express grief, for example, the worst approach is to look off into the distance, get weepy, and walk around agitated. That is nothing more than a comment on what you think grief is. When you really experience grief, it is a very quiet emotion. If you must find it for a role, then sit down in a quiet room and think about someone you knew and loved who is no longer with you. If your character is grieving over his wife of 30 years whom he has just lost, don't wallow around on stage in grotesque anguish, because it will come across as stale, bad acting. In life, we try not to cry. We try desperately to hold on, to keep from crying. We may shed a tear sometimes in front of someone extremely close to us, but we don't walk around crying in front of people because it is embarrassing. So when you are tempted to cry on stage, I would encourage you to try not to cry and see where that takes you. Play the behavior. Walk the room; pick up an item that she used to wear or use; pick up a picture of the two of you or one that she took that involved a joke you shared; look at a book left open or a knitting project never to be completed. Find the behavior that surrounds the feeling: the laughing, the sharing, the rolling back of time. Always play the action, the behavior. That will take you much further. The feeling will come on its own. In fact, you will not be able to stop it, and you will not need to "reach" to display it.

I must warn you: When your acting is purely intellectual, when the *what if* is rooted in thought rather than passion, the result is an uninspired and uninspiring performance. For instance, imagine again that you are cast as Hamlet, a role that calls for extreme action based on family honor and a son's love for his father. Perhaps you were not raised to place great value on such principles and do not respect either of them in your present, adult life. Well, then, you must ask yourself what is truly important to you. If the best you can come up with is a hope to see the end of global warming (or world illiteracy, or child abuse, or domestic violence, or even world hunger), then you are on the wrong track. As noble as this thought is, you cannot act it. Why? Because it is an *idea* and nobody can act an idea. Real people take extreme action out of personal passion, not intellect. Actors who fail to grasp this essential commandment may be doing their best, but sadly, their performances are dull.

Such actors are working from the head as opposed to the more emotional center. This is not what Stanislavski hoped for from actors. His vision was perhaps closer to Artaud's, which asked that everything that is dark and murky in the subconscious be exposed on stage. Artaud advocated that artists pursue such expression even if it meant destroying themselves. Stanislavski, on the other hand, did not believe in self-destruction. He never said, "Go mad; become the character." Unfortunately, however, there are actors who do just that and jump off the proverbial cliff without a parachute. Sometimes it is out of inexperience or lack of training. Sometimes it is out of self-indulgence. In any case, do you know what happens when you jump without a parachute? Very rarely do you fly. Stanislavski envisioned that his System would allow actors to use their conscious mind to reach the unconscious and, through specific behavior, arouse particular feelings from their own lives that are most analogous to the characters'.

Admittedly, this *what if* process can be unpleasant. If there is anyone reading this book who thinks that acting is one fun stage experience after another, think again. Do not be naive to the more unsettling side of your work. For example, there is a scene in this book that deals with suicide. Hopefully, you won't have experienced this feeling, but you should be able to use *if.* Actors need to stretch themselves to come as close as possible. A college freshman or sophomore needs to look at this and say, "Well, I don't know exactly what this is, but I've observed life. I'll try." After all, that is why you are in acting class, because you are drawn to the subject of human behavior. Maybe you remember that, at some time or other, you felt like saying, "If my boyfriend leaves me, I'll kill myself." Or, "I won't be able to handle it if I'm not admitted to that school." Now, the depth of isolation and loneliness in the character you will find in the "Fren and Joey" script (see page 32) far exceeds the typical young lover's sense of loss or the average applicant's hopes for college admission. But that does not matter, really. What matters is that you know what it feels like to be desperate enough to say, "I don't want to live if I can't have that." That is all you need to act the scene with confidence.

Similarly, you will find yourself sometimes asking *what if* when a role calls for a physical experience that you've never had: horrible pain, or intoxication. The scene "Pat and Mickey" (see page 44) requires that the actor work on drunkenness. With luck, no student cast in that scene will know the physical experience (or the emotional reality) of being drunk all of the time. If you have never been intoxicated, you will have to find something that works for you in the *if* department. You might ask yourself, "What would I be like if somebody woke me up suddenly, first thing in the morning, and tried having a conversation with me?" The answer might give you a departure point for the sort of foggy, half-conscious state that comes with being inebriated. Whatever you use, you must find something that takes you to that blurry place. And be sure that, whatever you use, you do not just "make it up," because that would involve only imagination. Admittedly, imagination is an important asset for any actor but, in and of itself, it is not enough to allow for truth to occur in the moment on stage. It must come from something real inside of you. You absolutely must work with an experience that you actually had or with a *what if* that is personal.

Now, is everyone an actor? Of course not, nor should everyone be. Although we all have emotions, it is important to acknowledge an individual's right to emotional privacy. Certainly there is nothing wrong with being the kind of person who is not interested in (or temperamentally suited to) accessing their passions. In fact, the world might go a bit mad if everyone chose to emote on a regular basis. So, if you really examine yourself, and decide you truly do not have strong feelings or the desire to express them, then you have answered for yourself whether or not you should be an actor. If you do not have real passion that you are willing to access over and over again, then you probably do not possess the basic stuff you would need to become an actor. I have met many fascinating and brilliant people who, once they found out what was really involved in acting, chose to pursue other interests.

Over the years, I have heard several performers claim (with a decided sense of defeat), "I can't do that. I can't honestly relate to that feeling or to the action the character takes in response to her feeling. And I can't find anything analogous in my own life." In my opinion, *I can't* always means, *I won't*. It is, when all is said and done, a matter of will. There are times in our work—whether because we are turned off by the role or because we are physically ill and not up to the task—when we have to garner our will and say, "I *will* do this. I *will* travel back through the recesses of my mind and my soul to find the analogous experience." In doing that, you meet the challenge inherent in acting. You answer the call.

A comforting word: When you are up against a tough role, tackling feelings that seem completely foreign (or even repulsive), take reassurance from the irrefutable fact that we are all human. We all have the same feelings in us. So even if you shock or horrify us, if you do it truthfully, you are simply reminding us of our own humanity.

Objective

Although the magic "if" is a useful tool, and while Stanislavski believed in its importance, it is not one of the three fundamental blocks of his System. Actually, he developed the System after years of frustration with his own acting. He wondered why the play connected for him on some nights but not on others. He began to ask himself some questions. As an actor, you must ask yourself these questions each and every time you begin work on a role.

1. What does your character want? (Objective)
2. What is the other character doing that prevents your character from having it? (Problem)
3. Given that particular problem, what action does your character take to meet the objective? (Action)

Out of this careful line of questioning, Stanislavski devised the System's three basic elements: Objective, Problem, and Action.

Objective is the term that Stanislavski used to describe the actor's intention, your goal on stage. One of the purposes of this book is to illustrate that, given the exact same dialogue, a scene can change depending upon each character's objective. In the "Lan and Lesley" scene, for example (see page 38), Lan returns from an evening out to find Lesley waiting. When Lesley's objective is to keep Lan dependent on their love, the scene unfolds in one way. When Lesley's objective, using exactly the same words on stage, is to put distance between them in order to be free of the relationship, then it unfolds in a very different way.

Just as there is a *conscious* objective—the character's conscious purpose—there is also an *unconscious* objective that the character does not understand or even recognize. But as the actor interpreting that character, *you* must know it in order to make your work dramatically interesting and bigger than life. When you act, you are not becoming that character. You are interpreting that character. And there is a big difference—for example, in a scene about ambition, an actor might very well have the conscious objective, "I want them to think that I am closer to getting the job than they are." But in truth, that will take her only a line or two into the script. In contrast, she could use: "In an effort to overcome my feelings of inadequacy (unconscious objective), I wish to prove to my rival that I have a superior chance of getting the job (conscious objective)." That will take her a lot further! Why? The first objective is an idea—wanting her rival to *think* something—that exists in her head. Aside from the fact that we cannot *act* an idea, or for that matter act with just our head, the first example does not give the actor enough to gain from the scene. The second example is active and more personal. In other words, no matter what the part, you must want something for yourself. If you do not, there will not be enough need and desire pushing you to utter your lines.

Acting, after all, is an abstraction of the self. That means there are two selves going. You have yourself, you, the actor, the person you are. And you have the self of the character. You must merge these two selves in a way that makes your lines in the script believable and truthful. The only way to do that is to give yourself a conscious objective, one that has to do with you, the real you, and that moves you to take action. Remember, too, that you must identify what you will have to overcome in yourself in order to reach your goal on stage. That is your unconscious objective. Formulate your objective so that it includes both the character's conscious and unconscious goal. Phrase your objective in the following way:

In an effort to overcome my feelings of inadequacy, (*unconscious objective*) I wish to convince my rival that I have a better chance of getting the job (*conscious objective*).

In an effort to overcome my fear of embarrassing myself by revealing too much, (*unconscious objective*) I wish to maintain emotional reserve (*conscious objective*).

In the effort to overcome my sense of superiority, (*unconscious objective*) I wish to remain anonymous to this stranger (*conscious objective*).

Another way to explain all this is to say that you do not want to use an altruistic objective. That is because self-interest is a fact of human nature. What about Joan of Arc, you might ask. Or Gandhi? Or Moses? Or Jesus? Even then, your objective should relate to self. Jesus did what he did because he needed to do it. He had great love for humankind. He even laid down his life for it, we are told. Still, he did what he did because it was his destiny. He wanted to do it. It was what he needed to do in order to feel right about himself. The same applies to Joan of Arc. Or Mother Teresa. Mother Teresa did not think she was a saint. She believed that she was doing what she needed to do with her life. Great heroes of war, calamity, or tragedy act out of reflex, but they are not shoved into it. They behave as they do because they deem it necessary and appropriate.

It is one thing to ask yourself, "What does the character consciously want?" It is quite another to really probe the issue. Each time you answer, ask yourself again: Why would the character want that? Eventually, you will get to an objective that the character is not aware of, but, as the actor, you need to be. For example, in Tennessee Williams's *The Glass Menagerie*, a play that explores tension between dreamers and cynics, we find a number of scenes in which Amanda's objective appears to be: "I wish to keep my son, Tom, in line because I don't want him to get offtrack." But an actor trained in the System has to ask herself why Amanda would want that. Without much difficulty, she probably would answer, "because I wish to inspire him to overcome the irresponsible behavior that I've seen in him." But, again, she must ask herself why Amanda has that desire. With some considered thought she might respond: "Because I wish to insure that he not behave like his father." Again, why is this important? After some more thought, she will likely find: "Because I wish to keep him and not be abandoned by him like I was by his father." And there you have it: Amanda's unconscious objective! Notice that, as you move from the conscious to the unconscious objective, you begin to see the reasons for Amanda's misplaced anger toward her son. Knowing Amanda's conscious objective is a helpful guide, but it is the deep-rooted, unconscious objective that gives you enough insight to bring Amanda to life for an audience.

If this process takes you to an unconscious objective such as, "Because I want to be happy," you have gone astray. That is too general. You want to find the specific. The objective needs to be immediate and right there in front of you. It has to be something that is taking place on stage. Do not be concerned with what you, as the actor, know is going to happen later in the script. In every single scene, you must want something from this person, or these people, there on stage with you. Bring all of your concentration to *that* spot, *that* moment.

Problem

Problem is the second of the main facets of Stanislavski's System. It translates into the question, What is it about the behavior of the other person (or people) on stage that prevents me from achieving my objective?

Problem is an often misunderstood part of the System. One way to simplify it is to remember that problem always has to do with the behavior of the other person on stage. The problem is not something about or within you. Many times I've asked actors, "What is your problem?" and they answer, "I'm afraid they won't like me," or "I wish to hide that I'm really trying to dupe them." However, these are not problems from a Stanislavski standpoint—these are inner concerns. Your problem always has to do with the behavior of the *other* character. For example, if you are determined to confront the other character in order to regain your control, while the other person is entirely preoccupied with other matters, you could describe your problem as "their distraction."

For another example, imagine a situation in which a parent reprimands his teenage son for behaving badly in public. If you were going to act in or direct that scene, you can clearly identify each actor's problem. If you play the father, your problem is your son's rebellious disregard for social conventions. If you play the son, your problem is your dad's anger.

One way to grasp the concept of problem, then, and to grasp the idea of action versus counteraction, is to see that each character's problem is the other character's behavior. Again, I would refer you to "Lan and Lesley" (see page 38). In one situation, Lan's problem is Lesley's jealousy. In another, the problem is Lesley's indifference. For the actor cast as Lan, these two very different problems produce very different kinds of behavior. In another scene, "Fom and Kad" (see page 52), one of the circumstances has Fom recently moved to a big city from a small town. Lonely, Fom's objective is to make a friend, so the character keeps trying to strike up a conversation, the way folks do back home. Kad, however, is a seasoned urbanite who fears strangers, because in Kad's experience they often have bad intentions. The objective for Kad, then, is to avoid danger by avoiding interaction. Thus the tension of the scene. Fom is up against a cold shoulder. As an actor, how do you work around that? And Kad must contend with a suspiciously pushy stranger. How do you protect yourself from that? In other words, each character gives the other a clear problem.

What would happen if Fom's objective were different? What if Fom wanted to fit in by imitating those who live nearby? By making this adjustment, in just one of the characters, the scene is destroyed. Why? Done this way, the scene would not have any tension—in fact, there probably would not be any dialogue in such a scene because, without a problem, neither of the characters would ever speak. It is watching you try to solve your problem that makes your performance exciting.

All of these examples show how interdependent actors are when they work together. They must give each other a problem in order to make their scene dynamic and meaningful. Young actors often turn to the script to provide their problem. This is a mistake for two reasons. First, there is more than one way to interpret any good script. (This is what makes it worthwhile to watch more than one production of plays like *Othello* or *The Homecoming*.) Even more important, to use the script as a guideline for establishing your character's problem is to deny your fellow actors the chance to bring their own artistry to the project. A simple clip of dialogue will help illustrate my point.

JESSE

How can you speak like this to me?

TIE

I'm doing this for your own good.

What is Jesse's problem? If you look to the script for your answer you might come up with "Tie's disrespect." Still, disrespect can take many forms. The real question must be: How does this actor demonstrate disrespect? Through cruelty? Through dismissing nonchalance? Through patronizing flattery? Whatever the answer, *that* represents your problem in the exchange.

And what about Tie's problem? A careful reading of the script might lead you to answer "Jesse's arrogance." Again, I would remind actors that arrogance has a multitude of faces. It is bravado in some; smug condescension in others. So the actor's job is to identify and respond to the specific problem that a specific actor chooses to give you. As you gain experience, you will come to value those acting partners with the intelligence and emotional depth to offer you complex and psychologically astute problems, because it is with these partners that your work will illuminate the furthest reaches of the human condition.

If your partner does not give you a problem, then you have nothing to do, really. In fact, when an experienced actor works with a beginner, this often happens: the novice does not know how to "get in the way." The result is a lopsided performance in which the experienced actor pretends to be solving a problem that is not evident. This leads to nothing but artificial acting. To avoid this, never pretend to be contending with a problem that the other actor is not presenting. Contend only with what you are given. The other actor's behavior is always your problem. So, if the worst happens and your partner's behavior gives you *no* problem, then your problem becomes this person's emotional catatonia.

Action

That leads us to *action,* the third principle of Stanislavski's acting System. Harold Clurman, founder of Group Theatre and one of the most respected figures in theatre history, said many times, "The first law of the theatre is action. The second law of the theatre is action. The third law of the theatre is action. Action. Acting. Actor." By *action,* in the System, we do not mean movement—we mean behavior. The "through line of action" describes your behavior. How are you behaving? What is the verb? The action is always a verb, and there are hundreds: *to intimidate, to charm, to deceive, to guide, to accommodate, to renounce, to irritate, to conceal, to surrender, to tolerate,* and so forth. There are subtle actions, such as *to adapt, to understand, to bear.* But we should never forget that we are always active when we are on stage, even in a passive situation. A good example of a passive action is waiting. If we wait for our lover, then our action might be to ponder the possible reasons for his lateness. If we are waiting for the executioner, on the other hand, our action would be quite different. The point is that we remain active on stage. We always have an action, and it is always a verb. Right now, as you read these words, your action is *to absorb;* you absorb whatever you can that helps you learn about acting.

When you have an objective, it is only natural to take different actions to achieve it. In this way, as in so many ways, acting is just like real life and the System mirrors the life force. For example, if you want to ingratiate yourself with your boss, you might flatter her, impress her with your knowledge, or even brag about where you went on your last vacation. You would try a few different tactics in the effort to reach your goal. If your problem is her disinterest, your behavior would be different than if your problem is her belittlement. All actions must come out of your objective, and all must acknowledge your problem.

It comes down to this: if the audience does not see the tension of opposing behaviors up there on the screen or stage, then they are probably not seeing the script the writer had in mind. Good theatre and good film demand conflict, and conflict can occur only through behavior, one character's behavior being different than another's. If one person is behaving in a specific way when you are together on stage, then it is incumbent upon you to behave in a way that generates conflict. The actor who understands that concept is ready to work.

When actors feel awkward on stage and do not know what they are doing, when they feel unbelievable or dishonest, almost invariably they are in this trouble because they do not know the correct action. It is a sad and sorry sight to see a poor actor standing there trying to look interesting, saying words. Clearly, this will not work. So, as Clurman said, the unending chain of command in our work is action. Pin the word on your dressing room mirror, engrave it on your brain, and more importantly, use it in your work.

Through line of action is the phrase given to the overall behavior of a character in a scene and also to an entire section of a script. Say that the plot calls for your character to seduce another character. This extends through the entire scene, from "Don't you want to sit down and have coffee?" to the final come-on. So the through line of action is *to seduce,* but within that scene there are also other actions, such as *to flirt, to lure, to amuse,* all of which lead to seduction.

So, how do you know when to change actions? When your partner gives you a new problem, your action changes. In a scene about seduction, if your acting partner is resisting your advances, you continue to use actions that revolve around the through line action *to seduce.* However, if your partner begins to succumb, you must shift actions in order to maintain the tension or conflict. If, in the midst of the seduction, your partner starts to threaten or frighten you, what then? Shift your action. Your problem has changed; therefore your action changes. You do not abandon *to seduce,* but simply find a creative action to help you accomplish it.

These smaller actions on the individual lines may vary as long as they logically apply to the through line. For example, if your through line of action is *to intimidate,* then within that action there will be other actions, such as *to confront, to demean, to accuse,* and *to demand.* All of these have to do with intimidating the other person. And the intimidating has to do with getting what you want, which in this case is probably control. Put it all together and you have the three elements of the System working in unison:

Objective: I wish to be in control

but . . . .

Problem: Their distraction or preoccupation

gets in the way, so . . . .

Action: I choose "to intimidate."

These, then, are the three components of Stanislavski's method. They are the tools we use to do our work. They allow us to lend clarity and resonance to our performance. This method serves the play because there is a natural abrasion inherent in drama; there are cross purposes that move the play along. Actors using Stanislavski's approach reflect this tension in their behavior. Can actors produce clear performances without using the System? Certainly, but only if the role is completely like themselves. Since this happens, at best, only once or twice in a lifetime, technique is essential. Stanislavski's System offers the actor concrete and specific guidance. If used properly, it will help the actor beyond measure.

One Last Word

Because acting is behavior, and because behavior has changed over the past hundred years, contemporary actors face a unique challenge. When we compare past performances with present ones, we realize how profound this change in behavior has been, and how specifically acting reflects this change. In 1900, a fine interpretation of Hamlet consisted of raving and tears. By 1950, Hamlet was more introspective and depressed. Today, Hamlet could easily be secretive, inexpressive, and bitter. Perhaps this is because we have all become more guarded. Most certainly, we are more restrained in expressing our emotions. This restraint has occurred in all of us, and the younger the person, the more pronounced it is. When an actor prepares, it must be from a personal place in their soul. And though the gifted actor knows not to force the expression of inner thought or feeling, it is in the nature of a talented performer to bring the unspoken reality to the surface. In order to express individual truth, the actor accepts the obligation of balancing these two opposing urges. When the actor is careful and gentle with the self, never pushing too hard or too fast, then the truth that rests in the actor's soul—the truth that is analogous with the character—is given a chance to come forth without demands liberated from excess, and free to reveal and express our universal humanity.

For all of you who wish to do this work, let me remind you that it is a great honor to be an actor. After all, there is something divine in creating a reality. So keep your eye on heaven. Turn your face to the sun.

Part II

The Scripts

Chris and Sage

Situation One

The Circumstances
These two people are complete strangers, alone together in a reception room. They talk casually until the mention of "tests." Then everything changes.

Sage's Objective and Problem
Lately, Sage has been overwhelmed with worry about the results of these tests. Over the course of the scene, we see that frustration and anxiety give way to anger. Thus the objective: **In an effort to overcome my feeling of isolation, I wish to agitate this stranger into sharing my point of view.** After all, misery loves company. So, actions can range from blowing up to challenging and, finally, to honestly admitting to the fear. Sage's problem is Chris's composure.

Chris's Objective and Problem
A considerate and even kind person, Chris is initially just interested in passing time by visiting with this stranger. But when Sage becomes upset, the objective becomes more focused: **In an effort to overcome my own fears about the test, I wish to make this stranger feel stronger.** (So the through line of action becomes *to reassure.*) Specific actions might be to tease affectionately, to comfort, to give "tough love," or to share deeply personal information. Chris's problem is Sage's extreme anxiety.

Situation Two

The Circumstances
These two characters are in a doctor's waiting room. They've been close friends for many years, despite the fact that Chris has always been more restrained than Sage would like. Now they both fear that Sage may have a terminal illness. All their actions and reactions come out of this fear.

Sage's Objective and Problem
Sage has always silently accepted the limits of Chris's cool temperament, not expecting more. But now, faced with the possibility of dying, Sage wants to get past all the limits on the friendship. The resulting objective is: **In an effort to overcome feelings of unworthiness, I wish to elicit a show of feelings from Chris.** The problem is Chris's emotional reserve.

Chris's Objective and Problem
Chris wants to support Sage but also wants to keep things from getting too high-pitched. The expression of emotion is difficult for Chris. So the objective is: **In an effort to overcome the fear of making a fool of myself by revealing too much, I wish to maintain emotional reserve.** The actions used can be to offer objective facts, to try calming Sage down, to agree, to encourage, even to teach. The problem? Sage's sudden need to talk about feelings.

Situation Three

The Circumstances
There is deep love between these two people. But in this scenario, it is Chris who is dying. Both characters know the medical facts, and the doctor visits are really for Sage, who doesn't seem able to accept the inevitable. Sitting in a doctor's reception area, the facade begins to crumble.

Sage's Objective and Problem

Sage's needs are obviously complex but overriding everything is the desire to hold on. Being reassured of Chris's love feels to Sage like their relationship isn't ending. So that becomes the objective: **In an effort to overcome feelings of being abandoned, I wish to force an emotional showdown.** Possible actions could include: to tighten the bond, to apologize, to distract. Sage's problem is Chris's detachment.

Chris's Objective and Problem

Chris has come to terms with dying. The disbelief, anger, and fear are gone. Chris has stopped fighting, and wishes Sage would silently accept the inevitable. Chris's objective: **In an effort to avoid the feeling of being overwhelmed by regret and loss, I wish to encourage Sage to be strong.** So actions might be to discount as unimportant, to explain, to flatter, to lovingly scold, to confide and, ultimately, to acknowledge the deep bond between them. Chris's problem is that Sage won't let go.

Tests

A waiting room in a doctor's office. Two people are waiting.

CHRIS

Any time now.

SAGE

I think so.

CHRIS

They must be running late.

SAGE

What time is it?

CHRIS

I don't know, but it doesn't matter.
They get to you when they're ready.

SAGE

Yes.

PAUSE

Tests and more tests. I wonder what
they do with all of those tests.

CHRIS

Well . . . I suppose they use the tests to
determine what they need to know.

SAGE

Why don't they tell you what they're looking for?

CHRIS

They assume you wouldn't understand. Do you think you would understand?

SAGE

I guess not. But I'd like to think they'd care enough to try to explain.

CHRIS

Sure.

SAGE

I don't know what I'm doing here. What good is it? Do you know what I mean?

CHRIS

I think so.

SAGE

It goes on and on and each day I really feel more and more helpless.

CHRIS

But you're strong enough to . . .

SAGE

I am not strong. I wish I were. You see,

if I were able to . . . oh please, I'm
sorry. I should never have started talking like this to you.

CHRIS

Sometimes it's good to talk. Go ahead. I
don't mind . . . not at all.

SAGE

But it really isn't right to burden you
with what I'm going through.

CHRIS

You're wrong. I'm just the person to talk
to . . . and it's not a burden.

PAUSE

SAGE

It's the parting from someone I love
that I can't stand. I can't stand that. I
don't know if I can do that. I don't
know if I can let go.

CHRIS

I won't pretend to know your feelings,
but I do believe if you are truly close to
someone, really love another person, you
can't be parted. By anything. You can
never "leave" them. Never. Not really.

PAUSE

Sage

Do you love someone like that?

Chris

Yes, I do. I do love someone like that.

Sage

Have you ever let them know?

Chris

I think I have. I hope so.

Fren and Joey

Situation One

The Circumstances
Fren and Joey used to be very close, but then Joey did something that deeply hurt and offended Fren. The actors should decide for themselves exactly what happened so that their images are specific rather than general.

Joey's Objective and Problem
Joey misses Fren and wants things the way they were. That gives a clear objective: **In an effort to overcome guilt, I wish to earn Fren's forgiveness.** So appropriate actions might be to roll back time, to bring back the good old days, and to genuinely apologize. The problem is that Fren rejects all of Joey's efforts.

Fren's Objective and Problem
Fren is still very hurt and that produces the objective: **In the effort to overcome feelings of unworthiness, I wish to make Joey feel the same pain that was inflicted on me.** (That may not be noble, but it's very human.) So all of Fren's actions—to dismiss, to make fun of, to mimic, to scold—are rooted in the effort to make Joey feel rejected. The problem is Joey's charm.

Situation Two

The Circumstances
Fren and Joey work together. Fren is a real nose-to-the-grindstone person who doesn't reach out to anyone in the office. Joey, on the

other hand, is the office linchpin, liked and respected for knowing everything and everyone.

Joey's Objective and Problem

Joey's objective is this: **In an effort to overcome feelings of power-lessness, I wish to get acquainted with Fren to find out what this office worker might know about the business.** Knowledge, after all, is power. So actions could include to cheer up, to look for common concerns, to commiserate, and maybe even to share secrets. The problem is Fren's aloofness.

Fren's Objective and Problem

Fren, who desperately wants to be appreciated for doing exceptional work, resents Joey's popularity around the office. Feeling overlooked and under-valued, Fren certainly isn't willing to share any information with someone who'll only use it to enhance his own prestige. The objective is: **In an effort to overcome the feeling of being undeserving, I wish to protect myself from this self-serving coworker.** Actions might be to withhold, to brood, to reject, and to challenge. Fren's problem is Joey's persistence.

Situation Three

The Circumstances

Again, Fren and Joey are coworkers but they rarely interact. Frankly, Fren is more interested in having a good time than in the nitty-gritty of what happens at the office. Joey, on the other hand, is incredibly lonely. In fact, if this effort to reach out fails, Joey plans to commit suicide.

Fren's Objective and Problem

Fren just wants to have fun without hurting anybody. Joey is odd, and this burst of conversation is totally out of character. It's even a little frightening. So Fren's objective is: **In the effort to overcome fears of being left out of the office social scene, I wish to reject the advances of this weird loner.** Actions might be to ignore, to politely dismiss, to imply some future get-together, or even to give superficial attention to Joey. The problem is Joey's vulnerability.

Joey's Objective and Problem

Joey wants to find a reason to go on living. Even one friendship would be enough. The resulting objective is: **In an effort to overcome the fear of the inevitable (loneliness, death), I wish to make contact with this office social butterfly.** So we should see Joey trying to find subjects of mutual interest, to invite, to agree, to compromise. Joey's problem is Fren's impersonal indifference.

In the Office

An office. Two desks.

JOEY

(Clearing the desk.) Well, that does
it. I'm finished.

FREN

(Still engaged in work file.) Hmnn.

JOEY

I had a lot to do today. It feels good to
be finished. It's nearly 5:30.

FREN

Sorry. Just a second.

JOEY

It's okay.

FREN starts to clear the desk. Finishing up, clearing up, slowly.

JOEY

(Watching Fren. Finally.) It's getting
dusky. I guess it's fall at last—shorter
days. Winter's on the way.

FREN looks up from clearing the desk.

JOEY

It looks a little breezy out there. Glad I
dressed warm.

FREN

Yes.

JOEY

It seems like the weather changed suddenly this year.

FREN

Did it.

JOEY

I thought so.

PAUSE

FREN

It's 5:30.

JOEY

Are you leaving? We could walk out together.

FREN

I'm not quite finished.

JOEY

That's fine. I can wait.

FREN

Well . . . I guess I could leave now.

JOEY

Want to have a drink or something?

FREN

Ah . . . I'd better not.

JOEY

We could talk.

FREN

I don't think so. I should go on . . .

JOEY

Please . . . I'd really like to.

FREN

I'm sorry. I just can't. I'll see you
tomorrow . . . So long . . .

FREN leaves hurriedly.

JOEY

Bye.

Left alone, JOEY considers it all, then gathers his things. Gets up
slowly and leaves. *(Note: Joey's final moment on stage is important.
Do not hurry it.)*

Lan and Lesley

Situation One

The Circumstances
Lan and Lesley have had a long relationship. Lan arrives home after having spent an evening being the center of a group's attention.

Lan's Objective and Problem
Although deeply committed to this relationship, Lan dreads the tension that's caused by Lesley's insecurity. Tonight has been perfect, and Lan wants it to end that way. So the objective is: **In an effort to overcome my fear of losing Lesley, I wish to minimize the importance of tonight's events.** Proper actions could be to include Lesley in the reasons for the evening's success and to minimize the attention. Lan's problem is Lesley's jealousy.

Lesley's Objective and Problem
Bright and passionately committed to this relationship, Lesley is afraid that Lan's popularity and success will jeopardize their bond. So Lesley's objective is: **In an effort to overcome my feelings of inadequacy, I wish to undermine Lan's confidence and plant seeds of self-doubt.** Reasonable actions might be to trivialize, to put on the defensive, to steal Lan's thunder. Lesley's problem is Lan's apparent humility about tonight's events.

Situation Two

The Circumstances
Again, these two people have a long-standing relationship but, for one of them, the thrill is gone. Again, Lan has returned from having

been out with a group of people, and is recounting the events of the evening. But here, Lesley is utterly indifferent to everything Lesley says and does.

Lan's Objective and Problem
Lan desperately wants to regain Lesley's love and respect, so the character works hard to be impressive. Lan's objective is: **In the effort to overcome my fears of not being loved, I wish to impress Lesley with my importance.** In the process, specific actions could include to boast, to brag, to repeat someone else's flattering comments. Lan's problem is Lesley's disinterest.

Lesley's Objective and Problem
Lesley truly wants to be free of this relationship. So the objective is: **In an effort to overcome my fear of hurting someone whom I no longer love, I wish to establish distance by appearing indifferent.** After all, indifference is the opposite of love. Actions might be to absorb the negative, to shun, to dismiss, and later to offer other options. Lesley's problem is Lan's clutching need to impress.

Situation Three

The Circumstances
Lan and Lesley work for the same firm and are competing for a major new account. Although they're both extremely talented, their professional styles are very different. Lan is direct and aggressive; Lesley is more cautious and methodical. When Lan returns to the office after an evening out with the prospective client, Lesley is still there.

Lan's Objective and Problem
Proud of the professional edge that this evening has offered, Lan wants to gloat and intimidate the competition. The objective is: **In an effort to overcome my fears of losing out, I wish to convince Lesley that tonight has given me the professional edge.**

Actions might be to brag, to exclude, to dominate. The problem is Lesley's serenity.

Lesley's Objective and Problem

Threatened by the advantage Lan may have gained, Lesley wants to know what happened with the client tonight. The objective is: **In an effort to overcome my fear that Lan will gain the upper hand by knowing too much about me, I wish to appear mysterious about what I know.** Actions could include: to plant seeds of doubt, to undermine, to withhold information, perhaps even to threaten. Lesley's problem is Lan's boastful confidence.

Waiting

LAN enters. LESLEY is waiting.

> **LESLEY**
>
> You're late.

> **LAN**
>
> Yes.

The following lines overlap.

> **LESLEY**
>
> Why ?

                as   **LAN**   says

> I'm sorry.

> **LAN**
>
> Strickland wanted me to go along.

> **LESLEY**
>
> Really.

> **LAN**
>
> We had to see them off . . . and entertain them with drinks and dinner first.

> **LESLEY**
>
> Sure.

LAN

We went to that new restaurant on the
boulevard—you know, with the awning
you mentioned. Not bad. We saw
Reilly—he'll probably tell you about it
tomorrow. So I'm telling you tonight.
Everyone seemed pleased that I'd come
along. They made a fuss about it. Quite
flattering really.

LESLEY

What did you say?

LAN

What do you mean?

LESLEY

Just now—what did you say?

LAN

I was telling you about where I was
tonight. Weren't you listening?

LESLEY

I was distracted for a moment. Tell
me again.

LAN

Well . . . I was saying that we went to
that new place . . . Fantango's . . . you
know . . . and I saw—never mind, it
isn't worth—

LESLEY

Yes? Worth what? Didn't you say
something about Reilly?

LAN

Oh yes . . . I saw—

LESLEY

(Interrupting.) He called here you
know. Tonight I mean.

LAN

Reilly did . . . ?

LESLEY

Yes, said he wanted to see me first thing
tomorrow morning.

LAN

Tomorrow. Well . . . isn't that
strange.

LESLEY

Yes.

LAN

Maybe he wants to tell you about
seeing me tonight.

LESLEY

Why would he want to do that?

Pat and Mickey

Situation One

The Circumstances

Mickey and Pat are old friends. Pat drinks too much, and is always at this same bar. This is not the first time Mickey has come along to watch out for Pat. In fact, it's a habit with them.

Mickey's Objective and Problem

A concerned and loving friend, Mickey tries to take care of Pat. Mickey admires Pat's specialness and finds it painful to see it buried inside a bottle. So the objective is: **In an effort to overcome my feelings of loneliness, I wish to get Pat reengaged in life.** Today, that means going together to watch a nearby parade. Specific actions might be to placate, to tease, to coax, to convince. Mickey's problem is Pat's defensiveness.

Pat's Objective and Problem

Pat undoubtedly has deep reasons for drinking but, at this point, they're long forgotten. Getting drunk is now just a way of life. That makes Pat feel insulted by anyone whose sobriety suggests superiority. So the objective becomes: **In the effort to overcome my feelings of past guilt, I wish to defend my present way of life.** Actions could include: to put off, to ignore, to disagree, to challenge, to ridicule. Pat's problem is Mickey's determination.

Situation Two

The Circumstances

Mickey and Pat are old drinking buddies, both of them relying too much on alcohol for a good time. They're also an odd match. Mickey is a jolly drunk, eager to have fun and act like a kid. Pat, on the other hand, gets drunk as a way to vent the anger that's too frightening to express when sober.

Mickey's Objective and Problem

Fairly drunk, Mickey just wants to have some fun! The parade sounds like a good time. There will be people around, and parades remind Mickey of childhood—when life was simple and responsibility was left up to the adults. Thus the objective: **In an effort to overcome great pain over the past, I wish to have fun and diversion by getting Pat to go to the parade with me.** Actions could include to amuse, to hint at, to tease, to plan, to convince, to plead, to nag. Mickey's problem is Pat's meanness.

Pat's Objective and Problem

Pat is a lost soul whose self-loathing and self-pity have combined to create an isolated drunk. The objective is: **In the effort to overcome my self-anger, I wish to attack anything positive around me.** Appropriate actions can range from: to insult, to demean, to make fun of. The problem is Mickey's carefree good nature.

Situation Three

The Circumstances

Mickey waits tables in the bar where Pat often comes to drink. They are attracted to each other but Pat's insecurity always seems to build a wall between them. Tonight, Pat has had a few too many and, as Mickey prepares to get off work, the two talk about going together to a parade.

Mickey's Objective and Problem

Mickey wants to charm Pat but doesn't want to take advantage of the situation. Maybe if they spend some time out in the fresh air, watching the parade, Pat would have time to sober up. Then a romantic evening might begin. So Mickey's objective is: **In an effort to overcome my insecurity about being desirable, I wish to convince Pat to come to the parade as a prelude to a possible romantic encounter.** Reasonable actions could be: to invite, to promote the idea, to flirt, to divert attention. Mickey's problem is Pat's reticence.

Pat's Objective and Problem

Basically a shy person, Pat likes Mickey, too, but doesn't want to appear foolish as a result of being drunk. As appealing as an evening with Mickey sounds, the chance of blowing it feels too scary. So Pat's objective is: **In an effort to overcome the fear of my crush becoming obvious, I wish to appear disinterested in the parade.** Trying hard to appear sober, Pat's actions might be to rationalize, to converse, to self-mock, to stall, to joke. The problem is Mickey's flirtatious appeal.

At the Bar

A bar. Two people.

PAT

Have a drink.

MICKEY

No, I'm fine thanks.

PAT

Well, I'm fine thanks.

PAUSE

MICKEY

You know, there's a parade in about thirty minutes—two blocks over— there's going to be a parade.

PAT

I heard.

MICKEY

There are probably still good spots, if a person wanted to see it.

PAT

Yeah.

MICKEY

I think there are going to be several bands.

PAT

Great.

MICKEY

Oh, you like bands.

PAT

Not especially.

PAUSE

MICKEY

Let's go see the parade.

PAT

Are you kidding?

MICKEY

We could get a flag. —Well, I guess no flag—but we could watch the bands march and play. Maybe, we'll see someone there you know. Or I know. Anyway, let's go.

PAUSE

MICKEY

What do you think?

PAT

I think bands and parades and flags and marching bands are for kids. Do I look like a kid to you?

MICKEY

You look like you could use a parade.

PAT

I'd like to finish my drink if you don't mind.

MICKEY

Hey, forget your drink. Let's go to the parade. You'll have a good time. You'll see. Forget your troubles. Come on.

PAT

Look . . . you're okay . . . You're okay to ask me to go with you . . . great even. But I'm not the parade type. Probably never was.

MICKEY

Well then, it's time you were. Hey, haven't you heard, "everybody loves a parade"?

PAT

Yeah, I've heard that.

MICKEY

Well, give it a chance.

PAT

I haven't been to a parade in quite awhile.

MICKEY

It's fine. All you have to do is watch. Come on, let's go.

PAT

I don't think I can.

MICKEY

Why not?

PAT

Because I doubt if I can stand up.

MICKEY

Sure, I'll help you. Hear the band music? We're going to the parade.

MICKEY starts to take PAT's arm to help.

PAT

You're really something.

MICKEY

There'll be uniforms and horns and drums and marching bands and a good time. You'll see.

PAT

You're really something.

PAT and MICKEY leave. MICKEY is helping to guide PAT.

Fom and Kad

Situation One

The Circumstances

These two people have never met, but they live in the same apartment building and have seen each other many times. Fom has a secret crush on Kad, but has no way of being introduced. The only possibility seems to be initiating a conversation about the pet dog that Kad frequently walks around the block.

Fom's Objective and Problem

Fom has a crush and wants to explore it. The objective, then, is fairly straightforward: **In an effort to overcome fear of personal rejection, I wish to initiate a conversation with Kad about the dog.** The dog is just a convenient excuse, a way to start a conversation. Specific actions might be to flatter, to amuse, to charm. Fom's problem is Kad's aloofness.

Kad's Objective and Problem

Fom's crush has not gone unnoticed by Kad who is also somewhat interested. Still, Kad worries about appearances. So the objective is: **In an effort to overcome my fear of being thought "easy," I wish to maintain my dignity by appearing aloof.** This behavior is common in shy people. Specific actions can be to condescend, to challenge (*line: "Excuse me."*) and even to ignore. Kad's problem is Fom's attractiveness.

Situation Two

The Circumstances
Again, these people are neighbors in a big city. Fom has recently moved from a small town where it's perfectly appropriate to strike up a conversation with somebody walking their dog. Kad, however, is a long-time urbanite who fears the motives of strangers.

Fom's Objective and Problem
Fom wants to be sociable, the way folks are back home. In that world, it's considered polite to notice a neighbor's dog. Having nothing but wholesome intentions, Fom's objective becomes: **In the effort to overcome fears of not fitting in, I wish to reach out and make a new friend.** Actions could be to initiate conversation, to flatter and to convey continued interest. Fom's problem is Kad's dismissing manner.

Kad's Objective and Problem
Convinced that only dangerous people start talking with you out of nowhere, Kad thinks Fom seems too nice, too friendly. Who is this person? Kad aims to play it safe. The objective is: **In an effort to overcome the realization that I am lonely and without friends, I wish to dissuade this stranger's advances.** Actions might be to ignore, to dismiss, to minimize. The problem is Fom's persistence.

Situation Three

The Circumstances
Kad's dog is dying and will be put to sleep tomorrow. So this is their last evening walk together. Sad over the impending loss, Kad's attention is focused entirely on the dog. Although a complete stranger, Fom can see that this is no typical walk around the block and, unaware of the particulars, wants to be of some comfort to a stranger.

Fom's Objective and Problem

Fom wants to ease this person's obvious distress (and perhaps even make certain that there's no emergency going on). Unaware that the pet is the very reason for Kad's sadness, Fom's tries to reach out by initiating conversation about the dog. The objective, then, is: **In an effort to overcome my own sadness, I wish to comfort this stranger.** Appropriate actions are rooted in generosity: to charm, to compliment, to cajole, to gently tease. Fom's problem is Kad's obvious distress.

Kad's Objective and Problem

Although touched by this stranger's kindness, Kad can't bear to explain anything. The character's objective is: **In an effort to overcome the feelings that come up each time I think about losing my pet, I wish to evade this stranger's questions about the animal and maintain my emotional equilibrium.** Actions might be: to fend off questions about the dog and withhold information—all the while remaining civil and polite. The problem is Fom's solicitousness.

Walking the Dog

Two people are standing on a street corner, waiting for traffic to allow them to cross. One of them, KAD, is holding a leash with a dog.

After a long PAUSE

> **FOM**
>
> That's a nice dog.

> **KAD**
>
> Hm . . .

> **FOM**
>
> I say that's a nice dog you have there.

> **KAD**
>
> Oh . . . yes.

PAUSE

> **FOM**
>
> Seems well behaved.

> **KAD**
>
> Oh, yes.

PAUSE

> **FOM**
>
> So, what's its name?

KAD

Excuse me?

FOM

I just asked what your dog's name is.

KAD

Oh, it's Harold.

FOM

What?

KAD

Beg pardon?

FOM

Did you say Harold?

KAD

Yes.

FOM

Your dog's name is Harold.

KAD

Yes, Harold.

FOM

Well . . .

Haser and Fondi

Situation One

The Circumstances

A national conference has brought together leading scientists from around the country. Haser is a renowned researcher who plans to use this out-of-town seminar as a way of meeting possible assistants for a new project. Fondi is a promising young scientist who desperately wants the job but who lacks the experience to be seriously considered. Spotting Haser in a hotel lobby, Fondi has to come up with some way of initiating a conversation.

Fondi's Objective and Problem

Fondi knows that working with Haser would ensure a brilliant career. An involvement in this project could open important doors and create unparalleled opportunities. The point, then, is to meet Haser and make a good impression. The objective is: **In an effort to overcome my fear of being thought ordinary, I wish to attempt and persist in this unorthodox method of introduction and interview.** Fondi is no fool, but a ridiculous plan is the only option. So Fondi stages a charade, opens conversation, changes the subject, confesses the truth, attempts to make a final impression. Fondi's problem is Haser's refusal to discuss professional matters.

Haser's Objective and Problem

Haser just wants to relax and enjoy some down time. Initially, Fondi's intrusion seems innocent enough: just a case of mistaken identity. But then too many questions are asked and Haser begins protecting personal and professional privacy. The character's objective is: **In an effort to overcome the fear of being thought smug and self-important, I wish to avoid this stranger's probing by appearing disinterested in talk of me or my work.** Specific actions might be to provide basic information, to not take things too seriously, to laugh off, to change the subject, to reprimand, to regain control. Haser's problem is Fondi's persistence.

Situation Two

The Circumstances

Again, Haser is a research scientist on an out-of-town business trip. But here, Fondi is a prostitute who regularly works this hotel lobby and approaches all potential clients by pretending to mistake them for "Toni(y) Morris."

Fondi's Objective and Problem

Confident and experienced, Fondi's objective is to solicit a client. The Morris masquerade is just a cover-up for the come-on and Fondi assumes that Haser understands that. When Haser bumbles the approach, Fondi wonders whether this is real naïveté or just a client wanting details. The objective is: **In an effort to overcome fear of failure, I wish to calmly seduce this inept scientist.** Actions might be to reenact a "come-on," to charm, to keep the conversation going, to entertain, to lure, to seduce, and eventually to calm. Fondi's problem is Haser's genuine ineptitude in this situation.

Haser's Objective and Problem

Shy and inexperienced, Haser is delightfully surprised by the attention of an attractive stranger. Although thoroughly attracted, the character certainly aims to maintain self-control. The objective is: **In an effort to avoid facing the fact that I am unsophisticated, I wish to appear in control of this situation.** Specific actions could be to register pleasant surprise, to self-efface, to ponder. Haser's problem is Fondi's overt sex appeal.

Situation Three

The Circumstances
This is an espionage scene in which high-security research information is to be traded for money. At this designated hour in this hotel lobby, the two operatives are to meet and transfer the classified data. Like all such encounters it must begin with the proper password.

Fondi's Objective and Problem
Fondi is an agent assigned to pay money for secrets. When the designated passwords, "Toni(y) Morris," fail to illicit the proper response, Fondi is on guard. Determined to get the data or expose an intelligence fraud, this character must balance a desire to complete the mission against the chance of a dangerous mistake. The objective is: **In an effort to overcome my fear of failure, I wish to maneuver the encounter to my advantage in order to succeed in my assignment.** Specific actions might be to pressure, to persist, to probe, and finally to at least keep the door open for continued interaction. Fondi's problem is Haser's diverted attention.

Haser's Objective and Problem
Haser is also eager to complete the mission, but "Toni(y) Morris" is not the opening cue this agent has been told to expect. So Haser chooses to reveal nothing. The character's objective is: **In an effort to overcome the fear of being duped, I wish to lead this stranger into revealing more.** Haser's actions are to conceal, to evade, to tantalize and to demand. Haser's problem is Fondi's mysteriousness.

In the Lobby

A hotel lobby. HASER is reading. FONDI enters. Approaches HASER.

FONDI

Toni(y) Morris?

HASER

(Looks up from reading.) What?

FONDI

Are you Toni(y) Morris?

HASER

No, I'm not.

FONDI

You aren't Toni(y) Morris?

HASER

No . . . There's the desk. They can probably help you.

FONDI

I can't believe I made such a mistake. I rarely do. In this case, I'm shocked that I made a mistake in identity. You look like the description I was given. Although, I hadn't expected Morris to be so . . . .

PAUSE

What are you reading?

HASER

Ah . . . something for my work.

FONDI

I see. I guess I disturbed you?

HASER

That's okay.

FONDI

I'm going to sit down for a minute
if that's okay.

HASER

I guess so. But don't you have to find . . .
Morris? Didn't you say you were looking
for . . . Toni(y) Morris?

FONDI

I don't care. I'd rather sit here awhile,
and visit with you if you have the time.

HASER

I suppose I do. It's fine.

PAUSE

FONDI

So, you said you were reading something for your work. What do you do?

HASER

I'm a research chemist.

FONDI

Oh.

HASER

I'm here in town for a short time
to interview prospective assistants.

FONDI

What will they do?

HASER

He or she will be my assistant in a
project for—

FONDI

A project? You mean a chemical
research project? That sounds like fun.

HASER

Fun?

FONDI

Well, I mean interesting. What is it?

HASER

Well, it's a highly specialized project for
the department of . . . Excuse me, but
it's difficult for me to talk about my
work. Not that you aren't easy enough
to talk to. But my work is very technical.
Understanding it is a challenge for me,
and I'm trained in it. So please don't be
offended, but let's skip the subject of my

work. Tell me what you do. Tell me
about your work. What do you do?

FONDI

Are you kidding?

HASER

Why, no . . . I'm not. What do you do?

FONDI

You mean you can't guess what I do?

HASER

What do you mean?

FONDI

Well, it seems pretty obvious, doesn't it?

HASER

Not to me.

FONDI

Come on, you know, don't you? I
think you knew the minute I walked
up to you.

HASER

All I know is that you were looking
for someone.

FONDI

Yes . . . I was looking for you.

HASER

Well, I'm flattered. What do you
want? . . . That is, why are you looking for me?

FONDI

That's what I mean . . . it's obvious . . .
don't you think?

HASER

I think you had better tell me. Now.

FONDI

Please don't get angry. I'm just doing
my work. Or trying to.

HASER

Work? Oh, I think I get it now. Well,
this is not the right time. Why don't
you leave your name and number at the
desk for me, and if I'm interested, I'll
call you tomorrow.

FONDI

I will. Please do call. I'm very good at
what I do. You won't be disappointed in
what you get. (Rises.) Thank you for
your time. I'll hope to hear from you.
(Exits.)

Padd and Roth

Situation One

The Circumstances

The head of a very wealthy family has died and the funeral brings together a number of heirs. As the family's attorney and closest advisor, Roth knows that, at such times, people can make foolish mistakes by trusting opportunists. Padd has known the family for years, always trying to finagle a place within its inner circle.

Roth's Objective and Problem

Cautious and even a bit suspicious by nature, Roth hardly views death as the time for turning to strangers, and intends to safeguard these highly-valued clients from any unseemly requests or overtures. So Roth's objective is: **In an effort to overcome my fear of losing status within the family as a result of this death, I wish to fend off this outsider who might threaten my position.** Actions might include to dismiss as unimportant, to warn, to confront, to brush off. Roth's problem is Padd's charming insistence.

Padd's Objective and Problem

Padd is a social activist who knew the deceased to be a cold-hearted miser. Padd wants to "make a difference" by convincing the heirs to share some of their wealth with charity. To do that, Padd must get past Roth. So the objective is: **In the effort overcome my feeling of not doing enough for the poor, I wish to find a way into the family through this trusted representative.** To do that, Padd must win Roth's approval. Suitable actions might be to charm, to impress. Padd's problem is Roth's excluding, even hostile manner.

Situation Two

The Circumstances
Meeting for the first time at a funeral parlor, Roth and Padd have little in common. They did both grow up in this small town, but Roth is a genuine free spirit who left many years ago. Padd has never been further than a few hundred miles away.

Roth's Objective and Problem
A true nonconformist, Roth never felt "at home" in this small town, but has no desire to stir up trouble. With private (but important) reasons for showing up to pay respect, Roth wants to quietly attend the funeral and then leave town again. So the objective is: **In the effort to overcome my sense of superiority, I wish to remain anonymous to this stranger.** Actions might include: to redirect conversation, to control conversation, to evade and to ignore. Roth's problem is Padd's friendliness.

Padd's Objective and Problem
Unworldly but truly kind, Padd is a friend of the grieving family and wants to offer comfort at this difficult time. The objective is: **In an effort to avoid my feelings of personal loss, I wish to extend myself to those attending the funeral.** For the moment, that means making this stranger feel welcome. Reasonable actions could be to inquire, to share information, to befriend. Padd's problem is Roth's evasiveness.

Situation Three

The Circumstances
Again, Roth and Padd are from this same small town and they've never met before this funeral. However, here it's Roth who has stayed behind and become the "town crier"—always knowing exactly who did what, with whom, and why. Padd, on the other hand, moved away years ago and, if appearance means anything, has done extremely well out there in the big world.

Roth's Objective and Problem

Out of a desire to be in control, Roth spends a lot of time keeping up on what happens in town. It's frustrating to be stumped by the appearance of this stranger. What could possibly be the connection to the deceased? So Roth's objective is: **In the effort to overcome my fear of losing control over my world, I wish to discover this stranger's connection to the deceased.** Virtually every action—to befriend, to charm, to inquire, to include, to seek commonality—comes out of a desire to solve the mystery. Roth's problem is Padd's secretiveness.

Padd's Objective and Problem

Years ago, and despite strong, overt family opposition, the deceased did something to help Padd move away and start a new life. Padd has not forgotten this favor and wants to pay final respects. Still, the character does not want to give in to sentimentality. The objective, then, becomes: **In the effort to overcome pangs of nostalgia, I wish to remain aloof.** Appropriate actions could be to withhold information, to dodge questions, and even to use Roth as a barrier from contact with other people. The Problem? Roth's nosiness.

Funeral

Funeral parlor. Two people.

ROTH

The family isn't here yet.

PADD

Do you know them?

ROTH

Yes.

PADD

I see.

ROTH

And you? You must be a friend.

PADD

Why do you think that?

ROTH

Because you're here.

PADD

Yes.

PAUSE

Some of the family must have come in
from out of town.

ROTH

One or two anyway.

PADD

Probably close relatives.

ROTH

Probably.

PAUSE

PADD

Do you live here in this town?

ROTH

I was born here.

PADD

You must know everyone around here
then. You probably know everyone.

ROTH

Well, I don't know you. You're not a
familiar face. I can't recall seeing you
around.

PADD

That's right. I don't know you.

PAUSE

ROTH

So, who are you?

PADD

I knew the deceased. This is a sad
occasion.

ROTH

Death always bring some sadness.

PADD

Yes.

ROTH

I believe the family is coming.
Excuse me.

PADD

Wait.

ROTH

I'm sorry.

PADD

Don't go.

ROTH

Excuse me.

ROTH exits.

Ash and Bolli

Situation One

The Circumstances

Ash and Bolli are performing in a play that's closing tonight. Ash is much less experienced and hangs on Bolli's every word. At the moment, however, Ash has something that Bolli wants: the phone number of an attractive fan who recently visited the cast back stage.

Ash's Objective and Problem

Completely in awe of Bolli's talent and with hopes of someday being just as good, Ash wants to learn as much as possible about what Bolli knows. The objective is: **In an effort to overcome my envy of Bolli's ability, I wish to learn how this artist works**. Specific actions could be: to acknowledge Bolli's superiority, to flatter, to ask for a deeper insight into the subject, to show off, perhaps even to pretend to understand. Ash's problem is Bolli's offhanded and even irreverent acceptance of the creative process.

Bolli's Objective and Problem

Although aware of Ash's respect and grateful for the admiration, Bolli takes acting for granted and tries to avoid conversation on the subject. At the moment, however, Bolli wants the phone number of an attractive fan, and Ash has it. So, Bolli simply aims to pursue a romance by charming this young performer into passing along the number. The objective becomes: **In an effort to overcome my sense of personal failure, I wish to avoid conversation about myself and, instead, secure Ash's help in having a good time**. Specific actions might include: to appear impressed, to tease, and to amuse. Bolli's problem is Ash's relentless focus on the work.

Situation Two

The Circumstances

Here, Ash is an ambitious director who's been hired to direct the newest production of this play that Bolli has starred in and studied for years. Unaware of Ash's deal, Bolli is out of work as of this closing night and has heard rumors about a new production. Ash is friends with the producer and Bolli would like a way of being introduced.

Ash's Objective and Problem

Ambitious but not yet established, Ash needs Bolli's help to solve the scene which is considered the crux of the play. At the same time, Ash does not want to reveal the upcoming project, much less make promises of an involvement in it. So the character's objective is: **In an effort to overcome my feelings of betraying a friend, I wish to flatter Bolli into sharing the solution that makes this play work.** Specific actions could be to assess Bolli's mood, to push for conversation, to flatter, to ingratiate, to simplify, to apologize. Ash's problem is Bolli's disinterest in discussing a play that's already closed.

Bolli's Objective and Problem

Having devoted the better part of a lifetime to acting, Bolli needs to go on working. The character knows that Ash could help by passing along that producer's phone number. So the objective is: **In an effort to avoid the feelings of failure that come with unemployment, I wish to narrow the experience gap between myself and Ash as a way of securing the phone number that could result in a new job.** Specific actions might be to tease, to be gracious, to try to maintain equality, to disclose. Bolli's problem is Ash's fawning insistence.

Situation Three

The Circumstances

Once again, we see two performers talking on closing night. Again, Ash is totally in awe of Bolli. But here, Bolli's passion for the stage has given way to a search for the spiritual. In recent months, Bolli has come to the decision to pursue the life of a mystic. At Bolli's request, Ash has learned of a retreat house several hundred miles away.

Ash's Objective and Problem

Ash would do anything for Bolli except, perhaps, take an active role in seeing this artist leave the theatre (even to the highest calling). So the character aims to convince Bolli that genuine talent is a rare gift, not to be abandoned. The objective, then, is: **In an effort to overcome my own lack of understanding of the artistic, I wish to rouse Bolli's sense of responsibility to the theatre.** Specific actions might be to praise, to draw someone out, to make someone feel needed. Ash's problem is Bolli's disinterest in artistic or worldly concerns.

Bolli's Objective and Problem

Bolli is consumed by a thirst for spiritual truth. In fact, after a long and successful acting career, the character yearns to pursue the life of a mystic. Hesitant to talk about tonight's stage experience because of its very personal nature, Bolli does decide to share it with Ash. The objective is: **In an effort to overcome my attachment to the world and to the theatre, I wish to impart the lessons I have learned from an even more profound pursuit.** The character's problem is Ash's attachment to their current relationship. To solve that problem we may see Bolli take various specific actions: to seek connection, to draw out, to minimize self, to share insight, to express gratitude, to use the language of the theatre to explain the spiritual. They all come out of Bolli's main objective: to leave this young student and friend with a last, profound lesson, that all great acting is the search for the soul.

Closing Night

Two people. Backstage dressing room.

ASH

It's closing night.

BOLLI

For sure.

ASH

Are you glad?

BOLLI

I don't know. Let me think about it.

ASH

You were great again tonight. And there at the end—that was different, wasn't it? You never did that before. Right?

BOLLI

That's right—I had never done it that way before.

ASH

I liked it . . . I loved it . . . It was inspiring.

BOLLI

Thank you.

PAUSE

ASH

What was it you were doing? I mean, what was the difference?

BOLLI

What did you see?

ASH

Well, it was as if you no longer cared what the others thought. You seemed to be thinking of someone else.

BOLLI

That's right.

ASH

Yes . . . but specifically, what were you doing?

BOLLI

I was acting.

ASH

Oh, come on. You know what I'm asking . . . that passion and . . . fire?

BOLLI

Are you trying to flatter me? If you are, you're succeeding. I'm deeply flattered. Now just forget it. Please.

ASH

Oh . . . well sure . . . sure.

PAUSE

ASH

I guess I was prying. I'm sorry. It's just that it was one of those rare moments.

BOLLI

(Smiles.) Will you stop?

ASH

Okay. Of course.

PAUSE

BOLLI

Are you packing up tonight?

ASH

Well, no . . . I have to come back tomorrow.

BOLLI

Really? Why's that?

ASH

For my things . . . and . . .

BOLLI

Oh, uh huh, I see.

SLIGHT PAUSE

Did you get that number?

ASH

I have it.

BOLLI

What is it?

PAUSE

ASH

I'll give it to you if you'll tell me what you were doing in that moment? Where were you?

BOLLI

You're kidding.

ASH

I'm not. I really want to know.

BOLLI

That's bribery.

ASH

It is. Please. Please tell me what happened. And how.

BOLLI

All right . . . I'll tell you, but I don't
want to ever speak of it again. Agreed?

ASH

Yes.

BOLLI

All right then. Tonight . . . for the first
time, I fully addressed my work to God
. . . and in the moment you are talking
about, I was in the closest communion
I have ever felt . . . Can I have the
number now?

ASH

Yes. Yes, of course. Sure. Here it is.

ASH hands a slip of paper to BOLLI.

Performance Rights